Mack

MACKEREL SALAD

By Ben Rogers

With an introduction by
Tamar Yoseloff

THE EMMA PRESS

for fathers, and fathers of fathers

THE EMMA PRESS

First published in Great Britain in 2016
by the Emma Press Ltd

Poems copyright © Ben Rogers 2016
Introduction copyright © Tamar Yoseloff 2016

ISBN 978-1-910139-41-7

A CIP catalogue record of this book
is available from the British Library.

Printed and bound in Great Britain
by Letterworks Ltd, Reading.

The Emma Press
theemmapress.com
queries@theemmapress.com
Birmingham, UK

Introduction

Ben Rogers' poems chronicle those passing moments which are made significant for having been noticed. Like another poet of the passing moment, Elizabeth Bishop, Rogers is always precise, ensuring that his readers see exactly what needs to be seen. His keen eye is trained on the ordinary – a teaspoon, a houseplant – objects which may not seem attractive enough in themselves to warrant a poem, but become so in Rogers' generous and expansive scope. Like Bishop, Rogers is reflective, considered, so that the noticed detail is simply the beginning of a wider exploration.

Take for example the teaspoon in the eponymous poem, which is being sought by an unnamed protagonist to stir sugar into his tea at 2am. Rogers places us in a youth hostel in Broken Hill, Australia, the location revealing lurking dilemmas. We never know if the man in search of the teaspoon is a resident, although we assume he is, nor why he has ended up there. Rogers' description creates a character who is haunted, possibly violent – '…sweat bubbling his brow, a red / wash over his skin, his white T- shirt stained' – but by the end of the poem, he becomes a subject for empathy. It is not until the last line that the narrator arrives: "A spoon is all he needs. I hand it over." In this small gesture, addressing a seemingly simple but endlessly complex need, there is a connection.

Connection is the thing that makes us human, conscious. The title poem, 'Mackerel Salad', is a tour de force on the act of decision-making, an examination of the myriad choices available to us in a day, or indeed, in a lifetime, one action leading to the next. The poem is from the point of view of an individual going about his day, but Rogers is careful to omit the first-person pronoun, so that we too can take on the persona of the decision-maker. Each small choice pushes us towards one which ultimately may have greater impact, and so the poem eventually steers us to a realisation of the precariousness of our lives; we hang on by the thread of the moment, but we are too wrapped up in what we should have for lunch or in staring into our phone screens, and we neglect to notice. Even in the midst of the city, with its clocks and schedules, 'the wind can't decide where it's going'.

Rogers is interested chiefly in the human condition, and how we rail against circumstance, the inconveniences of modern life, left as we are with the feeling that there should be more consolation, whether in religion or nature, but sometimes just in expressing what seems ineffable. Take for example the final lines of 'Hideout', in which Rogers is describing the movement of a windmill; in the end, it becomes something more elemental, crucial:

the lulling sweep of machinery
that some might call nature, or inevitability, or loss.

The poems in *Mackerel Salad* present a stand against indifference in a world that presents us with indifference. Rogers shows us the world we thought we knew, which, when we weren't looking, somehow became a little less familiar.

Tamar Yoseloff
MAY 2016

Contents

Moon Jellyfish

is the name given to thoughts, fat and changeable,
that have a kind of aloof machinery to them. You,

by which I mean you not everyone, might be indifferent
to the idea of someone attempting to articulate the feeling

they get when they sense their shadow is somehow
held up, as though a tendril of it has been caught

in a door that was closed too quickly, or maybe
compromised by the complicated silhouette of a cloud

that's got jammed in the sky by a sluggish
wind. Your indifference, by no stretch a deep-down

feeling, is a small organism, perhaps scooped into
existence by someone's interrogative glance that

felt in a way parental, and has a thin membrane
to it that means it could easily jumble into any number

of other drifting dispositions. When you look at it
though, twisting slowly in a syrup of midnight, you

cannot not consider how easily aesthetics, by trumping
all else, can become the slinkiest of anaesthetics, although

in thinking that you're also aware that, if someone
held a lamp over you, four squat bulbs flooding

your head from crown to collar, you wouldn't stake
your life on it. You wouldn't stake anything on it.

Teaspoon

Broken Hill Youth Hostel

The sugar jar stands open, waiting, and now
he needs a spoon, tea not table, to stir,
to blur the mirrored disc of his drink,
reflecting strip lighting, his face, the dark
of 2am. He's rattling drawers, all
the wrong ones, sweat bubbling his brow, a red
wash over his skin, his white T-shirt stained,
he just wants to whirlpool his tea, a small
want. His big frame slopes, unseen animal
perched on his shoulders, he soothes the mug's side,
talks of where men start on you out the blue,
fisticuffs, handing out black eyes for free,
leaving another slumped cold in the road.
A spoon is all he needs. I hand it over.

Mackerel Salad

Turned left out of the room, and returned for the security
    pass.

Conversation about pass, do you need it to get out.

Should it be possible for a building to require you to
    need a pass to get out.

Pressed button to get into stairwell and then because the
    light was flashing alternate green and orange you
    didn't need the pass to get out.

Turned right out of the building, many going the
    opposite way.

Crossed the road to a traffic island, thought about the
    odds of getting hit by a truck.

Odds increase of getting hit if you're thinking about
    something else while crossing, including thinking
    about the odds of getting hit.

Crossed the road from traffic island to other pavement,
    saw an advertisement for mortgages.

Pros for mortgages: the image of yellow flowers on a
    wooden countertop. Cons for mortgages: the
    word *mort* means death and *gage* means count.

Momentary contemplation about the countdown to
    death while passing a man with dice on his tie.

Entered the usual café and bought the mackerel salad,
    served by a woman with glasses who didn't quite
    make eye contact while smiling so was actually
    smiling at some air space.

Took the mackerel salad to a square in front of a church,
    thought about wavering prayer and murmuring
    candles.

Consideration of the paving arranged in circular
    patterns.

Started to pace round the square following the circular
     patterns, stepping on the individual paving slabs
     and not touching cracks.
Are they assembled to cater for some sort of ritual.
Do they reflect some sort of astral cartography.
How did Pluto feel when it was told it was not a planet.
Pluto doesn't feel things, because it's elemental.
Thought that it's hard to know that for absolutely sure.
Decided to ring a friend, and it went straight to
     answerphone, a recorded woman's voice neither
     of us know.
Didn't leave a message because of having heard sound of
     own voice on previous occasion and it sounding
     like someone else.
On that basis you might not speak at all.
Decided on a bench, sat on the right hand side nearer
     the coffee stall and ate first fork of mackerel salad.
Man at the coffee stall recommends the white chocolate
     and cherry flapjack to a woman in a dark red coat,
     but she doesn't buy it.
Thought about the different reds, thought about
     predators in fairy tale.
Read on phone an old post from days ago about someone
     giving up using their phone for the day the next
     day, although they will still use the internet.
Thought about being in a wilderness where phones
     won't work.
The wilderness had parched olive trees and powdery
     dirt, as well as stagnant water and reeds nearby –
     to the right and up a narrow path, if you can call
     it that, on the left.
The woman said earlier that this was the last day of the
     salad.
Thought that some last days go without you noticing, is it

better if you notice. Recalled the air conditioning unit in gated car park of a building south-west from the square towards the river, how when passing it it used to have a ticking sound that created the sense time was running out.

The last few times it has stopped ticking.

The sky isn't a mackerel one because the clouds are too large.

The wind can't decide where it's going.

Brigid's Cross

At the end of the first month of the year, which
for some people is the point when they are weakest,
you are supposed to tie three-legged crosses

twisted from green rushes so as to protect your
cowshed or cottage from all types of evil. Is this
why we are now surrounded by flower beds full

of black tulips opening their mouths to speak,
and overlooked by a series of chimneys that appear
to be coloured the blood of wild creatures?

And is this why the children that are here are huddled
under chairs, trying to use their hands to hide their heads,
even when it's their hands that give them away?

That Was Then

Grandfathers rip five-pound notes before our eyes.
We watch halves drift to sheepskin rugs.

In parks, we get scared at tops of metal arches.
Fathers say not to worry even though falls can kill.

Butterflies sail through gardens. They seem happy,
but die in days. We slice earthworms on slabs.

On nights of December 21sts we fear monsters.
We see hands in curtains, feel claws in beds.

Fathers of fathers collapse in bathrooms.
We picture last breaths on mirrors.

Grandmothers at seaside huts ask if we prefer
mothers or fathers. We shrug, murder crabs.

Mothers cry at feet of staircases.
We hug them, tell them it'll be ok. Lies like these help sleeps.

Birds fly into spare bedrooms. They crash into walls
and ceilings. We fly in dreams to get away from strangers.

Through the nights, trains rattle past ends of gardens
carrying nuclear wastes. Sheds blow over fences.

Faces in dark rooms applaud as we blow out candles.
But candles are lives and birthdays are deaths.

A Space Azalea

*'This azalea sprouted out from a seed of azaleas that had travelled
in space with a medical doctor and the first Japanese woman who
had explored space' (sign in courtyard of Matsumoto Castle)*

The absence of things, a plant shedding

a scattered signature of red. The name –
        something about remembering home.

In embryo, it had sensed its planet,

a dot smeared on a vast plane, the patch
        of crust where, free

from spinning in the frameless dark,

it would land, reconstitute and grow,
        unbend its stalk, start pandering to the sun,

set root. It's an *a*, not a *the*, other

pieces may be elsewhere, outside
        this immurement, walls famed

for their blackness. Black in the way space is not.

Bright Angel Trail

Grand Canyon, Arizona

The sun has blowtorched all cloud.
Mules can mean stamina, mules can mean victim.
The man who's gone said that you shouldn't attempt
                  to go to the bottom and back in
    the same day.
Another man who's gone said that he did it and it was
                  no problem.
As you go down, you are entering the photograph you
                  took at the top.
At the top you have your photograph taken
                  posted at *the edge of the world*,
    except it isn't the world and the world has no
        edge.
Seems an irony for an angel to lead the way down
                  but you can't have down without
    up.
Someone in the past said that if sun poured through
                  cracked cloud it was God.
The woman who walks down the first stretch of about
                  thirty zigs and partnering zags
    talks about education.
She's not sure if people learn what they should learn.
Gentle incline means a cocktail of zig-zag and mule.
At one point she reveals how a mouse's brain
                  is similar to tickertape and
    wonders how far it would stretch down the trail.
If you'd lost the thread in a labyrinth, you'd follow the
                  mice.
The path of least resistance is down, so that continues.
You don't know you've reached your limit until

you've passed it, so the point at which
you break isn't chronicled.
When the girl was on the ground you waited, you sat
her in the shade, the last time you
were here.

The man that squats next to you says *get out and get out*
quickly, words where you realise that
in matters of importance vocabulary is
small.
On the one hand you can start to walk back up the slope
but feel as though your head is
floating and on the other you can curl up by a
rock that's the size of a separated head.
The memory of exclamation marks and capital letters.
The American Indian said *well you are the hiker*,
and when he said it you thought how
am I a hiker.
Heat doesn't know anyone is anything.
Somewhere it makes a difference to someone if
you feel your head is spinning
clockwise or anti-clockwise.
A man passes whom you spoke to several days ago
somewhere else, and he pauses
afflicted by the duty of recognition.
Maybe it would make a difference if you were south
of the equator.
He walks on, saying he has to *get on*.
Pouring water over your head from the bottles in your
bag.
The man who said you had stopped sweating has
gone.
The American Indian kind of half-smiled, it's not clear
if it was for you or at you.
You conceive each step as a musical note,

each note is a step.
Zigs and zags multiply when you're not looking.
There could be an invisible hand on your shoulder,
                    and you wouldn't know it.
The soft tremor of heat, the stretched desert
                    of forehead.
Water runs off your head and writes a message
                    you can't translate in the obedient
      dust.
A labyrinth has no dead ends, and yet is one long
                    dead end.
The girl eventually made it, but sank multiple vodka
                    shots and didn't want to talk about it.
The man you never met whose car was parked near the
                    ridge didn't make it, and sank in sight
      of the car.
Looking down on the heads moving to and fro,
                    a pendulum of small blotches.
Victory is just loss deferred.
At some point dust doesn't get cut down
                    to smaller dust.

Hideout

Inside the treehouse, its ailing white paint, the ladder
that is now unclipped. In the cellar's dimmest corner,

under a discarded door on its side that now leads

to no specific room. In the accidental park near the railway
bridge, behind the defunct trunk of an oak defeated

by an unplanned storm. In an unlocked garage, beneath black

sacks of compost, belonging to the house at the end of the cul-
de-sac a half mile away. In the windmill on the heath, if they'll

welcome you in, listening to giant hands that forever turn

in the same direction, the lulling sweep of machinery
that some might call nature, or inevitability, or loss.

Searching for a woman in Fes

That way. He takes the coin, returns to dice
and I follow the trace of his finger through

a large arch, a yawn of blue and gold, down
streets cut like rivers, so old they've dropped

names, stamped out by the heavy tread of mules.
I know you're here. Children scatter like seeds,

little puffs of spice, one stepping up,
chiming out *chips and gravy, chips and gravy,*

as though imaginary food will solace the lost.
He leads me (not for free) down gaunt alleys,

where walls lean in, shedding scorched skin
and then he's gone, just dust, orange peel, the wail

of fourth prayer. I pass stalls sloped with garlic,
coils of fabric, the odd head of camel, to reach

a chair, feeling steam melt from sticky mint tea,
the out-of-tune fuzz of a television fizz on my ear

and watching the hand of a man playing dominoes,
tapping his temple as he stubs out a dead end.

carta marina

The carta marina is a 16th-century Scandinavian map of the seas, featuring a variety of sea hazards including whirlpools and mythical beasts

i

the cloven tail of coast clopped
heart of coast what you don't
know can hurt you barraged rump
of coast the sea ransacks it
with its iron wing the map tells
you where you might be your
route an index finger of nervy
pencil the compass doesn't
know where to look as when
it's an invisible claw of stone
that jabs your boat into depression
wood begins its downward sigh
rain's rough guttural the sound
accompanying as moth-eaten cloud
and leftovers of sun peer on
the shifting grey scales the sea
is awash with spit and tooth

ii

each wave a spilling mind
      trying to predict the next

instalment the future
      is a broken eye the future

is muck and salt the future
      is a giddy serpent whose

mouth and appetite exceed
      you and your vessel with

one tatty limb the sea juggles
      itself horizontal

and vertical swap places
      a hasty demolition of sound

iii

the moon is a charred swab land has become
a forbidden room land has become a persistent
drought fortune could favour you if you've
no courage whatsoever the pulsing rock
on the horizon that is land flickers in and out
of being a bird a bird cannot talk until it can
the water is a puzzle with no rules waves crack
the way that skin cracks the water is a book
endlessly re-writing the ending when the bird
speaks it has a heron's lips and taps the centre
of the map it tries to cajole your cracked psyche
one of the waves amidst this herd should drift
the way home you just have to catch it and then
you can sleep the sea is forever constant the sea
is never constant the sky questions your every
move you question the sky's questioning
the sky pelts you with hail

Voicemail

The elm & lime & ash leaves won't be still. The five men sitting around a four-sided table keep swaying & bobbing up & down as they speak, & they don't stop speaking. Nearby, the man in the checked shirt sitting opposite the woman in the blue dress is fondling his glass while it's got beer in it, & when it doesn't have beer in it he goes to the bar to set up another one. The woman can't resist tapping into her phone either a message or searching online for something relating to the message she is sending, or one she might send later. Elsewhere your mouth is moving & your ears are moving. Two other men, one bald with glasses & one bearded without, are standing & uncomfortable with their arms so they keep moving them, by crossing them or picking up a bottle, or putting down a bottle, or sucking their hand as though it's just been bitten & they need to tease out some toxin that might enter their bloodstream, or by abruptly pointing at each other or a direction that suggests the presence of something, in order to emphasise a point. Their latest point delivered with rabbit eyes is how accomplished the saxophonist was and how he constantly moved his mouth. The black plastic bags tethered around the tills outside won't rest. The sun is nervous about its persistent descent & so won't take a breath from its persistent descent. The river is forever crafting a new ripple.

Vogue Gyratory

'How the present complicated system offers any advantages is beyond easy comprehension. It makes one wonder if the planner responsible was power mad' (Brighton Bits blog post)

a

An unseen voice concludes *progress is progress.*
When passing, sometimes there's the dilemma
between the two adjacent crematoria, the one further
up the hill or the one nearer its foot. One has a better
view, the other is less effort, though both criteria
are arguably redundant. At the base of the hill,
the gyratory, a washing machine of cars in the middle
of which is a man washing his car, a brushed aqua
Yaris. The sun sliced by chimneys, a dying head-
lamp. The phrase hasn't been updated yet.

b

No glamour about the latest gull's performance
singing its throat out from the ridge of The Bear
Inn before crafting a series of improvised
swerves and dives towards the marina. The sun
has mutated into a mandarin that's been kicked in the gut.
You can't, unless a machine, draw perfect circles.
The clock that used to watch over a factory line's
spool of pills now points down on a five-bagged woman U-
turning back into Sainsbury's to collect the local paper
telling her that the big wheel might be chopped.

c

Past last orders and the car lights are six-point stars
that zip round a circuit not unlike a waltzer. The shape
is perhaps akin to an amoeba, a supposedly simple
organism. You might ask it the question *Why do*
you make life so complicated? and it might, like you did,
find the word *so* a cruel emphasis, and wonder what
else it could have done. Maybe it would respond
by saying simplicity isn't exactly in fashion.
A man steps up to draw cash from its heart
so he has the requisite fuel to drive round it again.

Exeunt

Returning from the bathroom, he finds the lounge freshly vacant,
still warm with *bonhomie*: a small pyramid of cigarette ash

settling itself in a geometric cut-glass dish, flutes of cherry
prosecco birthing bubbles, a wipe of candy lipstick shining

on the rim of one, a bent-back paperback breathing itself
into shape again, the partition into the dining room sticky

with finger-prints at thigh-height of chocolate parfait, a demure berg
of cork bobbing in a half-drunk merlot, an errant faux-pearl

button upturned and winkled behind the ankle of the taupe newly-
upholstered armchair. The talk of how much the chair cost yet

hangs in the air, along with the comment of the woman from down
the road that his responses were *most salient*, a mere moment

before he'd excused himself to then wonder, while he relieved
himself, while he glanced at the smiling family trio snapped

and clip-framed on a plane of damp sand, what she meant by *salient*.
He now sits on the edge of the ruby chaise longue, watches

the television mutely pedal down the closing minutes of the year, silent
fireworks spraying over the city, bouquets of unsmellable colour,

the camera panning slowly over a dark ocean of faces he doesn't know,
as they traipse through a song they don't know.

Monstera Deliciosa/ Semantic Satiation

The sort of plant someone might grip a name on, a name
lodged on a bath's corner ledge. A trickle from the pot,
shot with loam. Each leaf is an open hand with gaps
between the fingers, which suggests a loose hold on money,
and which could connect to having a blank with names.
A name that doesn't make you think of cheese. The plant
is a disorder that hangs over you, a shadow over a sheet
of water you cannot name, a shade you associate with
the metallic weight of regret. In the mirror, your face
has a tug to it you don't want to name. There's a folly
to the multi-feather-duster effect that the fronds have
as your father parades the plant down the hall on a plate
whose pattern you don't have the wherewithal to name.
The plant has achieved a size where it can no longer perch
and has been delivered to a new home behind the television,
there being no name like home. The television is in the room
named the living room, to distinguish it from the other
rooms. The fire reaches out to feather the guard. If the fire
were solid you'd name it a bed of thorns. Your mother
prods for a new channel, but before she does the news
broadcaster with a name you can't name announces
the death of a name you can't name who appeared in a show
with a name you can't name. The leaves reach out to smother
the television. The carpet's name is soft earth, the wallpaper's
name is mountain slate, the ceiling's name is a heart turned
to ice. The next trivia question in order to win a slice
named a cheese is to name the plant in the corner. Another
time, the plant there will be named a Norwegian spruce.
The window's names are outside, reality, growing up
and danger. This time though, the plant is unnameable.
Your parents have left the room, and you are left on the sofa

with your name, a word that reflects you but you see
through. A glass word and a plant that can't nurse.
You imagine the plant will move again, and in years
to come will plunge its many feet into hills spun with pine
and flint. Returning again to your name, it's not your name
anymore, and doesn't even taste like a name, let alone
name like a name.

Acknowledgements

Thanks to the editors of publications where poems in this pamphlet have previously appeared, including *Magma, 14, Transom*, and the anthology *New Poetries VI* (Carcanet, 2015).

I am also grateful to the poet Tamar Yoseloff for writing the introduction to this collection of poems.

Thanks also to Clare Pollard, Roddy Lumsden and the Wednesday Group poets for their advice and support, and to everyone who has given guidance or feedback on any of the poems in this pamphlet.

About the poet

Ben Rogers lives and works in London. He studied English at Cambridge and Film/TV Studies at the British Film Institute, specialising in East European animation. His poetry has been published in journals and anthologies, including *Magma, 14, Long Poem Magazine*, the Emma Press's *Slow Things* and Carcanet's *New Poetries VI*. Previously, he has also written the script for a puppet show, and a radio sketch show that aired on BBC London.

The Emma Press

small press, big dreams

The Emma Press is an independent publisher dedicated to producing beautiful, thought-provoking books. It was founded in 2012 by Emma Wright in Winnersh, UK, and is now based in Birmingham. It was shortlisted for the Michael Marks Award for Poetry Pamphlet Publishers in both 2014 and 2015.

In 2015 we travelled round the country with Myths and Monsters, a tour of poetry readings and workshops aimed at children aged 8+. This was made possible with a grant from Grants for the Arts, supported using public funding by the National Lottery through Arts Council England.

Our current publishing programme features a mixture of themed poetry anthologies and single-author poetry and prose pamphlets, with an ongoing engagement with the works of the Roman poet Ovid. We publish books which excite us and we are often on the lookout for new writing.

Sign up to the monthly Emma Press newsletter to hear about our events, publications and upcoming calls for submissions. All of our books are available to buy from our online shop, as well as to order or buy from all good bookshops.

http://theemmapress.com
http://emmavalleypress.blogspot.co.uk/

Other Emma Press Pamphlets

GOOSE FAIR NIGHT, *by Kathy Pimlott*

ISBN: 978 1 910139 35 6 – PRICE: £6.50

A generous, jellied feast of a book, full of sharp yet tender details
about friendship, family and familiarity.

TROUBLE, *by Alison Winch*

ISBN: 978 1 910139 39 4 – PRICE: £6.50

This book looks at different kinds of intimacy and what they can
reveal about sex, power and care.

TRUE TALES OF THE COUNTRYSIDE, *by Deborah Alma*

ISBN: 978-1-910139-26-4 – PRICE: £6.50

Deborah Alma writes vividly about sex, love and ageing, reflecting on
her experiences as a mixed-race, British-Asian woman.

OILS, *by Stephen Sexton*

ISBN: 978 1 910139 03 5 – PRICE: £6.50

Belfast poet Stephen Sexton evokes melancholy and a strange
romance throughout *Oils*, the 2015 PBS Spring Pamphlet Choice.

MYRTLE, *by Ruth Wiggins*

ISBN: 978 1 910139 12 7 – PRICE: £6.50

Ruth Wiggins celebrates the primal forces of nature and the human
heart in her heady debut, which is full of dry humour and wisdom.